QUEEN

LEGENDS

ALPHABET

Words by Robin Feiner

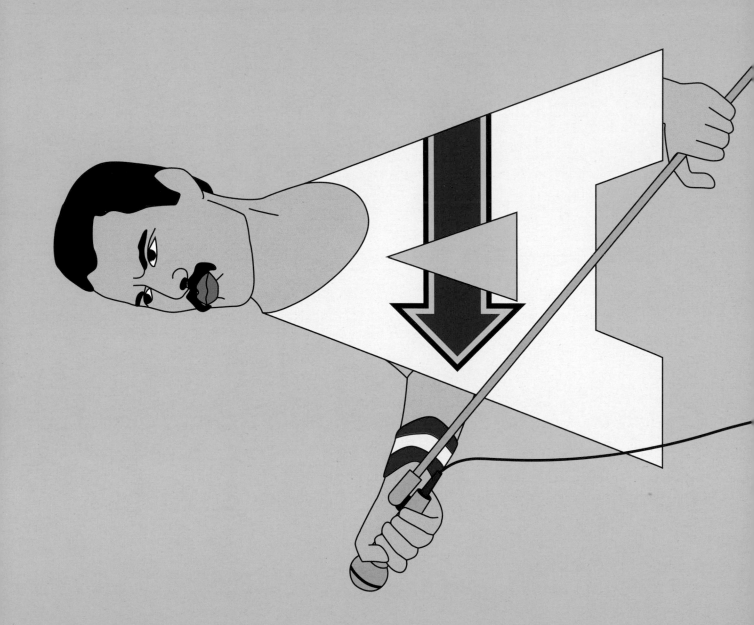

A is for Another One Bites the Dust.

This megahit, written by legend John Deacon, always leaves everyone hanging on the edge of their seat. Released in 1980, the track skyrocketed to the top of the Billboard 100 List, where it stayed in the top 10 for a total of 15 weeks.

'And another one gone and another one gone!'

B is for Bohemian Rhapsody.
Can you sing along to arguably the most legendary song of all time? 'I see a little silhouetto of a man, Scaramouch, Scaramouch, will you do the Fandango!'
This immeasurable rock opera masterpiece has been streamed billions of times and is the third biggest-selling single ever!

C is for I'm in Love with My Car. Taylor wrote the lyrics for this song, inspired by a roadie's love for his Triumph TR4. Sure of the song's potential, Taylor locked himself in a cupboard until Mercury agreed to make it Bohemian Rhapsody's B-side. And that car revving at the end of the song? That's Taylor's Alfa Romeo.

Cc

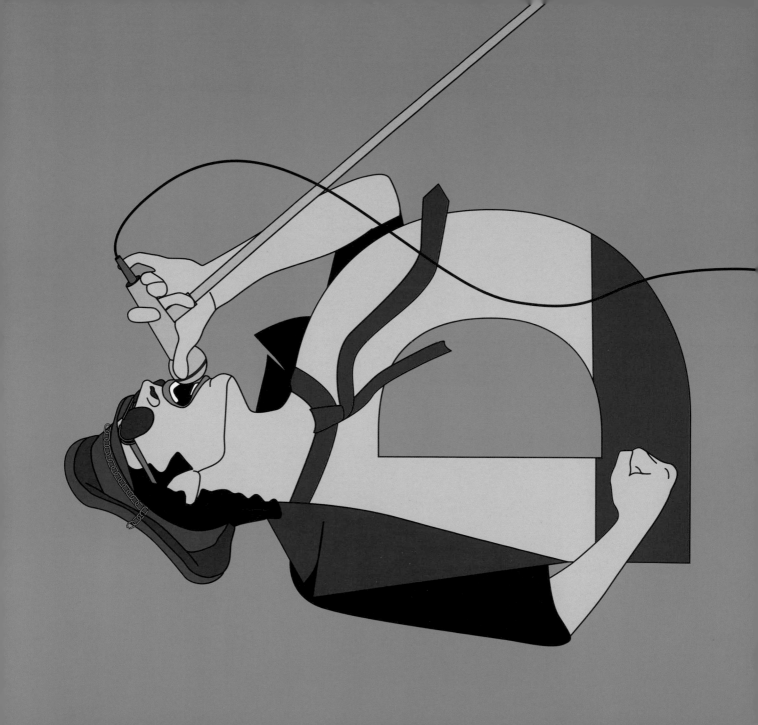

Dd

D is for Don't Stop Me Now.

Are you having a good time?

How could you not when

you're listening to Mercury's

whimsical piano crescendo?

This smash hit was released

on Queen's 1978 album Jazz.

It quickly became one of

their most legendary songs,

even making it onto their

1981 Greatest Hits album.

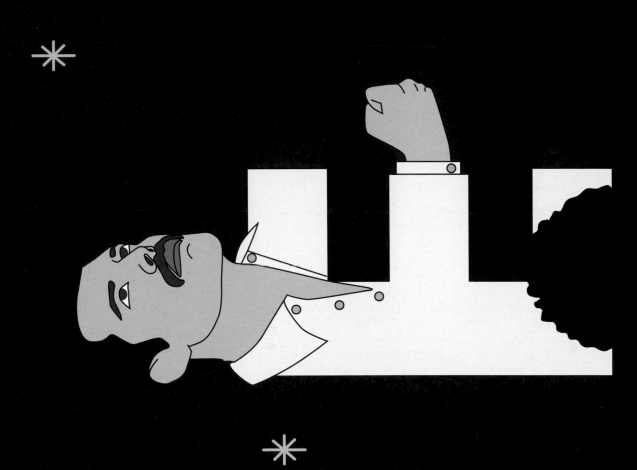

E is for Heaven for Everyone. While this emotional ballad was originally recorded with Freddie Mercury, it became somewhat of a love note to him after his death. Released posthumously in 1995, it instantly charted across Europe. The music video is one of Queen's most legendary, as it pays touching tribute to Mercury.

Ee

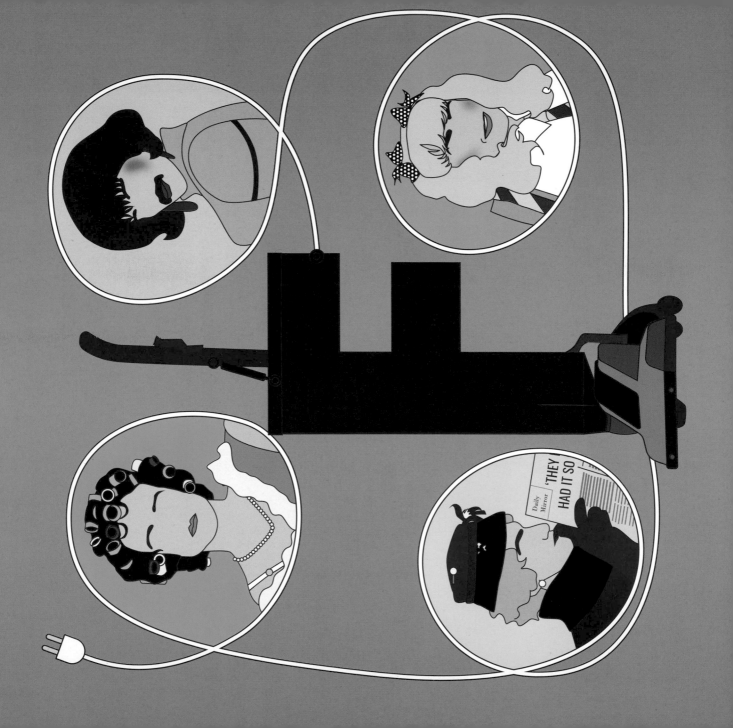

F is for I Want to Break Free.

One of Queen's most enduring songs, I Want to Break Free is a story of breaking away from a bad relationship. In some countries, it became an anthem with a political message for harsh dictatorships. No matter which way it's taken, this song makes an empowering statement.

G is for Radio Ga-Ga.

'All we hear is radio ga ga!' Taylor originally titled this song Radio Ca Ca in criticism of modern radio. After the band asked him to rewrite it with a positive spin, it became a nod to radio's glory days. It even inspired the name of one of today's most iconic singers, Lady Gaga.

H is for Now I'm Here.

On Queen's 1975 album Sheer Heart Attack, the band wanted to showcase their rock 'n' roll roots. Now I'm Here, which opens with some legendary guitar work and chorusing, made clear that Mercury and Queen were one of the best rock groups around.

Hh

I is for Innuendo.

6½ minutes. That's how long this epic gem lasts, and the music ranges from hard rock and opera to orchestra and flamenco guitar. The iconic song started as a jam session with Taylor, May, and Deacon when Mercury joined in with lyrics and a melody. Legendary...."'til the end of time.

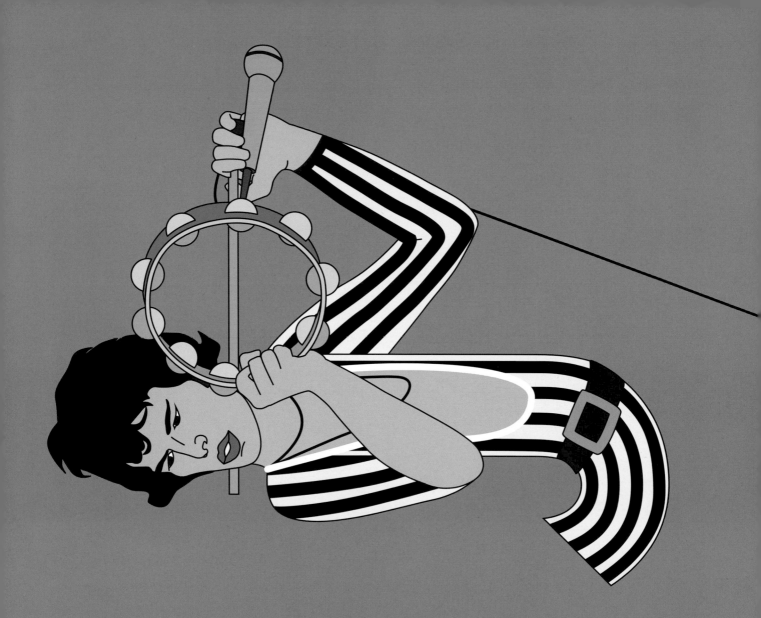

J is for Jazz.

Ranking Queen albums is an impossible ordeal. But to many, Jazz is easily one of its greatest compilations. Legendary songs like Don't Stop Me Now, Bicycle Race, and Fat Bottomed Girls all charted high on the Billboard 100.

Jj

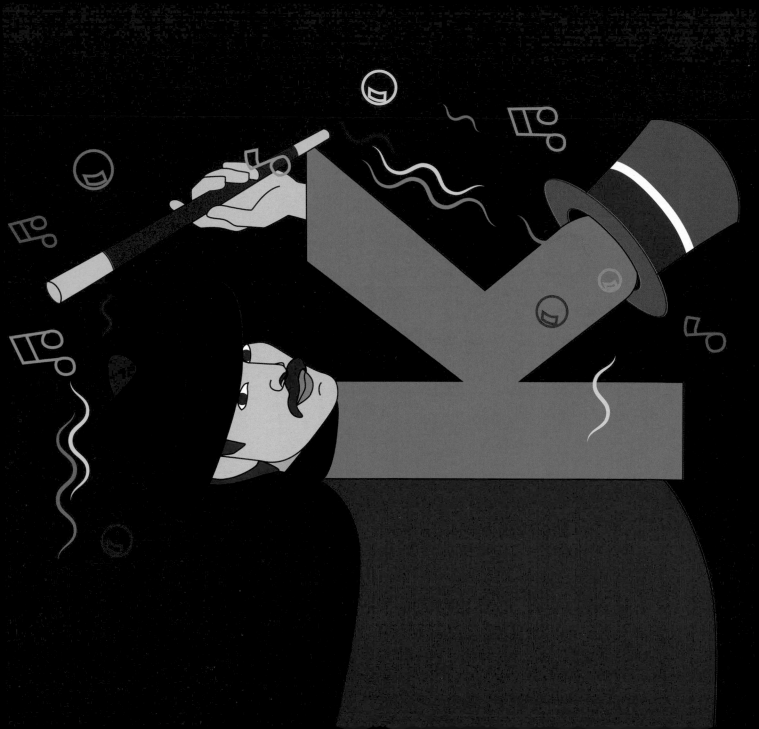

K is for A Kind of Magic

Taylor wrote this song's lyrics based on a line from the movie Highlander. The rest of the band followed with their own touches. The result? 'One prize, one goal... a kind of magic!' Sadly, the tour for this album proved to be Mercury's last.

K k

L is for Somebody to Love

Using multitracks of their voices, Queen created the impressive sound of a 100-person gospel choir for this tune. Inspired by Aretha Franklin's soulful music, Mercury wrote what he considered his best lyrics about a man searching for love. The result? A showcase of his love for gospel R&B.

Ll

M is for You're **My** Best Friend.

Bass guitarist John Deacon, a notorious recluse, penned this track for his wife. 'Ooh you're my best friend, ooh, you make me live!' Have truer and more passionate words ever been sung? The legendary love ballad has since been featured in countless movies with friendship themes.

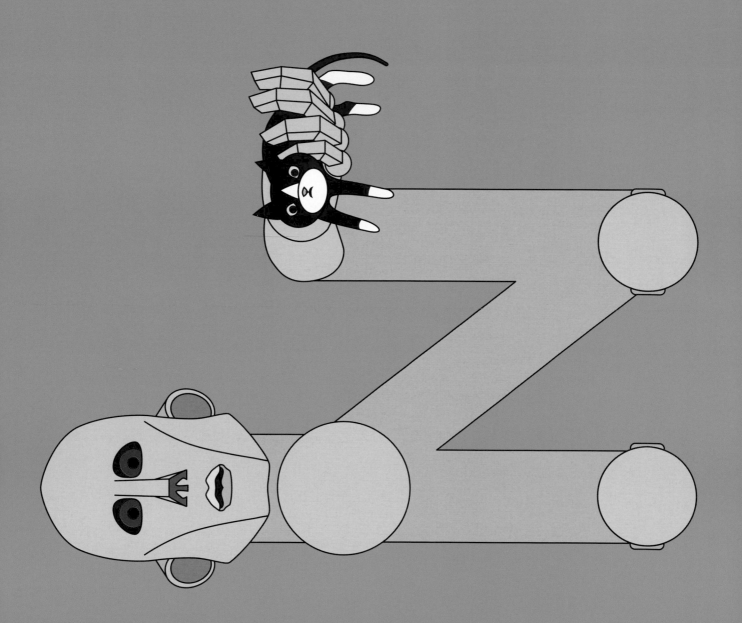

N is for News of the World.

Featuring the crowd-rousing classics We Will Rock You and We Are the Champions, this album became a staple for every Queen fan. But what really set it apart was the unique cover: a giant robot, created especially for Queen by sci-fi artist Frank Kelly Freas, creating chaos with the band.

O is for Good Old-Fashioned Lover Boy.

Written by Mercury, this track was featured on Queen's 1976 album, A Day at the Races, before being released as a single. Particularly noteworthy are May's legendary electric guitar flourishes, which come in well-timed waves to accentuate the Lover Boy's romantics.

P is for Play the Game.

For a long time, Queen refused to use electronic instruments. That all changed in 1980 with their hit album The Game. On this opening track—written by Mercury for one of his former lovers—they embraced synths in legendary style and returned to making 'epic' songs.

Q is for Killer Queen.

Undoubtedly Queen's break-through hit, this legendary 1974 single from Sheer Heart Attack announced their arrival. The world said hello to their whimsical attitudes, clever songwriting, grand harmonizing, and most of all to Mercury's unparalleled nature. "Let them eat cake!" Indeed.

R is for Bicycle **Race**.

'Bicycle! Bicycle! Bicycle!'

It comes as a surprise to no
one that this 1980 classic is
the most-downloaded song
of all time about bicycles.
The simple-yet-catchy lyrics
were written one day while
Mercury was in France,
as Tour de France riders
sped by his window.
The rest is history!

Rr

S is for The Show Must Go On. This song became a commentary on Mercury's life. The lyrics showcase the flamboyant singer's attitude as he faced the future with marked determination: "I'll face it with a grin—I'm never giving in—on with the show!" Today, Mercury's ethic and legendary legacy live on!

T is for Who Wants To Live Forever.

Every so often, Queen switched up its catalog with a slow-burning masterpiece. Such was the case with this legendary operatic 1986 hit. Though the movie this song appeared in—Highlander— had little box office success, the tune itself lives on in the hearts of Queen fans....

forever!

U is for Under Pressure.

What happens when you put two of the greatest singers ever—Mercury and Bowie—in one room? They create the stuff of legend! Released in '81, this song about overcoming pressure vaulted to the top of the UK Singles Chart and has cemented its place in musical history as an anthem.

Uu

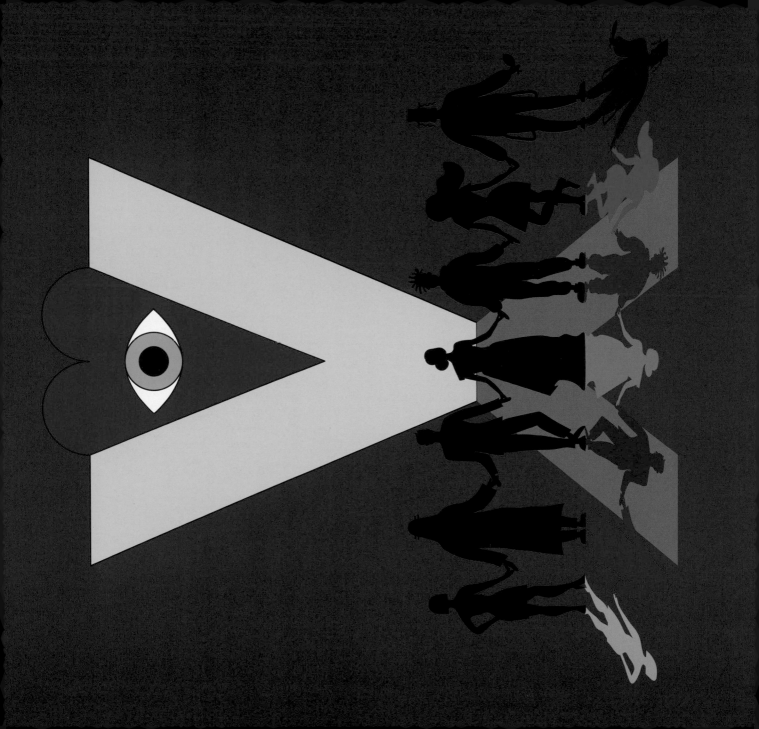

is for One ision.

This 1985 classic, included on A Kind of Magic, was inspired by the legendary life of one Martin Luther King Jr. The lyrics hammer home King's everlasting vision for racial harmony: "I'm gonna tell you there's no black and no white, no blood, no stain, all we need is one vision!'

Vv

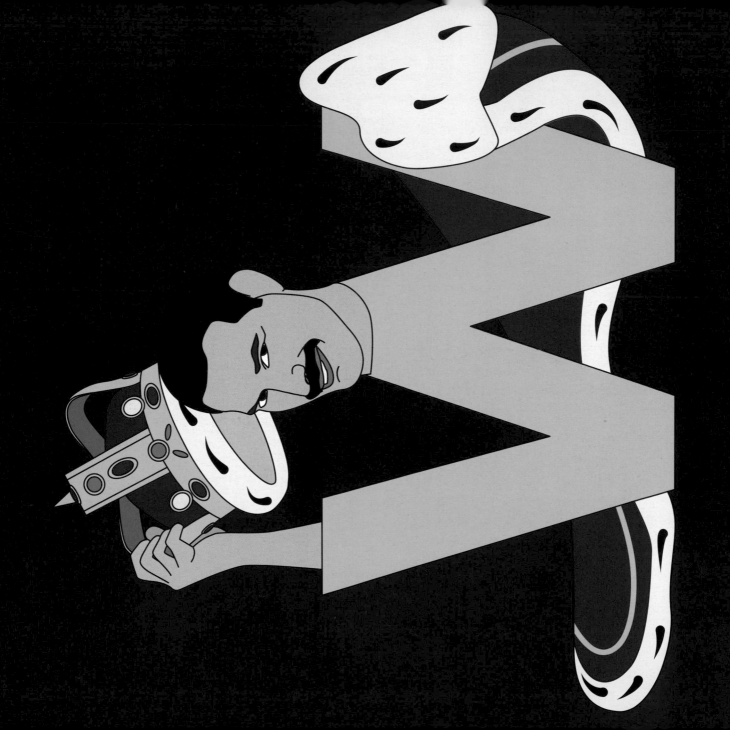

W is for We Are the Champions. There is no greater anthem, no song that will get an entire stadium rocking quite like this 1976 hit. When it debuted, it instantly charted in the US, UK, and Canada. Written by Mercury while watching soccer, it's now chanted by sports fans across the globe any time their team emerges victorious.

Ww

X is for Thank God It's **X**mas.

Taylor and May collaborated on the lyrics for Queen's only Christmas song. Mercury, who adored the holiday, immediately loved it and recorded his beautiful, understated vocals in Munich while working on his first solo album. "It's been a long hard year; thank God it's Christmas."

Xx

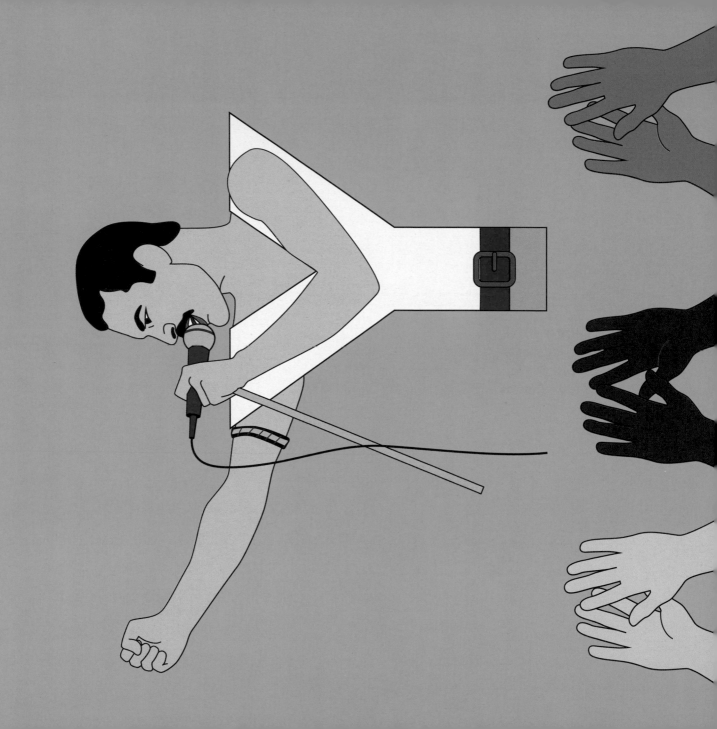

Y is for We Will Rock **Y**ou.

Queen's most popular song? That title likely belongs to this 1977 megahit off their News of the World album. Written by May, it is regarded as one of the greatest songs ever by Rolling Stone Magazine. It was also the second-to-last song played at the legendary Live Aid concert in '85.

Z is for Crazy Little Thing Called Love. Freddie Mercury wrote this classic—one of Queen's ultimate dance numbers—whilst taking a bubble bath. Viewed as a homage to Elvis, 'Crazy Little Thing Called Love' became Queen's first song to hit number one on the US Billboard 100 charts, where it then remained for four weeks.

Zz

The ever-expanding legendary library

QUEEN LEGENDS ALPHABET
www.alphabetlegends.com

Published by Alphabet Legends Pty Ltd in 2022
Created by Beck Feiner
Copyright © Alphabet Legends Pty Ltd 2022

Printed and bound in China.

9780645487039

ALPHABET LEGENDS